Profiling and Utilizing Learning Style

JAMES W. KEEFE, EDITOR

National Association of Secondary School Principals
1904 Association Drive, Reston, Virginia 22091

NASSP Learning Style Series
Learning Style Theory and Practice (1987)
Profiling and Utilizing Learning Style (1988)
Cognitive Elements of the Learning Style Profile (Fall 1988)
NASSP Learning Style Assessment Model (1989)

Executive Director: Scott D. Thomson
Director of Publications: Thomas F. Koerner
Assistant Director of Publications: Carol Bruce
Technical Editor: Eugenia Cooper Potter

National Association of Secondary School Principals
1904 Association Drive, Reston, Virginia 22091
(703) 860-0200

Contents

Contributing Authors

JAMES W. KEEFE is the NASSP director of research, chairman of the Learning Styles Task Force, and a principal co-author of the NASSP Learning Style Profile.

CHARLES A. LETTERI is an associate professor of educational psychology, director of the Institute for Research on Teaching and Learning Skills at the University of Vermont, and a member of NASSP's Learning Styles Task Force. He is a contributing co-author of the Learning Style Profile.

BARBARA FERRELL is an assistant professor in the department of psychology and philosophy at Texas Woman's University, and a member of NASSP's Learning Styles Task Force.

JOHN M. JENKINS is director of the P.K. Yonge Laboratory School at the University of Florida, Gainesville.

object, or attitudinal criteria—about what to do with a given message. It may reject the information, memorize it for short-term recall, transform it to conform to prior messages, or learn it by integrating, assimilating, differentiating, or associating it in working and long-term memory. The end result is a changed cognitive structure for the individual.

Cognitive styles are controls that are intrinsic to this information processing system. These cognitive controls, in turn, are influenced by various motivational biases and environmental preferences that the individual brings to learning. The gestalt of cognitive, affective, and environmental elements is what we term learning style.

The Task Force reviewed a large number of cognitive/learning style and brain behavior characteristics before establishing a developmental list and agreeing on operational definitions. During 1982-83, the group reached consensus on a multidimensional view of style with "learning style" as the umbrella concept and some 40-50 elements to be investigated. The Task Force decided that a new learning style instrument should be developed—a real state-of-the-art assessment tool.

Research Agenda

The Task Force adopted a research model of style proposed by Keefe (1979). This model views "learning style" as an umbrella term encompassing cognitive, affective, and physiological/environmental dimensions. (See Figure 1.) The Task Force's research agenda proposed to identify and review style elements in each of these dimensions.

Before proceeding with its research agenda, the Task Force developed a set of working definitions for a multidimensional view of style.

- *Learning Style* is the composite of characteristic cognitive, affective, and physiological factors that serve as relatively stable indicators of how a learner perceives, interacts with, and responds to the learning environment. It is demonstrated in that pattern of behavior and performance by which an individual approaches educational experiences. Its basis lies in the structure of neural organization and personality which both molds and is molded by human development and the learning experiences of home, school, and society (Keefe and Languis, 1983).
- *Cognitive Styles* are the information processing habits . . . which represent a person's typical modes of perceiving, thinking, remembering, and problem solving (Messick, 1969).
- *Affective Styles* are motivational processes—attention, expectancy, incentive—viewed as the learner's typical modes of arousing, directing, and sustaining behavior (Keefe, 1979).
- *Physiological Styles* are biologically-based modes of response that are founded on sex-related differences, personal nutrition and health, and accustomed reaction to the physical environment (Keefe, 1979).

The Task Force reviewed a lengthy list of cognitive/learning style and brain behavior characteristics before settling on a limited number for further study. The initial list included some 40 broad elements of style.

- Analytic vs. Nonanalytic
- Analytic vs. Global
- Reflective vs. Impulsive (conceptual tempo)
- Tolerance for Incongruous Experience
- Complexity vs. Simplicity
- Breadth of Categorization
- Focusing vs. Scanning
- Leveling vs. Sharpening
- Perceptual Modality Strengths/ Preferences
- Representational Capacity
- Mnemonic Construction Ability
- Attentional Biases
- Sense of Time (past, present, future)
- Simultaneous vs. Successive Processing
- Thinking Skills
- Need for Structure
- Conformity vs. Self-Direction
- Locus of Control (internal vs. external)
- Persistence
- Social Motivation
- Level of Anxiety
- Level of Curiosity
- Control Awareness
- Achievement Motivation
- Cooperation vs. Competition
- Need for Mobility
- Sound Preference
- Lighting Preference
- Temperature Preference
- Preference for Formal vs. Informal Environment
- Time of Day Preferences (morning, afternoon, evening)
- Intake Needs
- Cognitive Mapping Dimensions
  — Theoretical symbol meanings
  — Qualitative symbol meanings
  — Cultural determinants
  — Modalities of Inference
- Myers-Briggs Typology Dimensions
  — Judgment vs. perception
  — Thinking vs. feeling
  — Sensing vs. intuition
  — Introversion vs. extraversion

Ultimately, 20 elements of style were selected for investigation. Task Force members conducted careful searches of the literature and the existing instrumentation for each of these elements.

1. Perceptual modality strengths/preferences
2. Field independence-dependence (analytic vs. nonanalytic)
3. Simultaneous-successive processing (information processing tendencies)
4. Focusing-scanning (attention deployment)
5. Inductive-deductive (conceptualizing styles)
6. Reflective-impulsive (conceptual tempo)
7. Complex-simple (cognitive complexity)
8. Narrow-broad categorizing (equivalence range)

9. Sharpening-leveling (memory styles)
10. Active-reflective orientation (extraversion-introversion)
11. Thinking judgment-feeling judgment (decision-making values)
12. Social motivation (socio-cultural determinants)
13. Anxiety (arousal and activation)
14. Need for structure (conceptual level)
15. Achievement motivation (need for achievement)
16. Risk taking-cautiousness (tolerance for ambiguity)
17. Persistence
18. Time of day preferences (circadian rhythms)
19. Environmental elements (sound, light, temperature, formal-informal)
20. Need for mobility

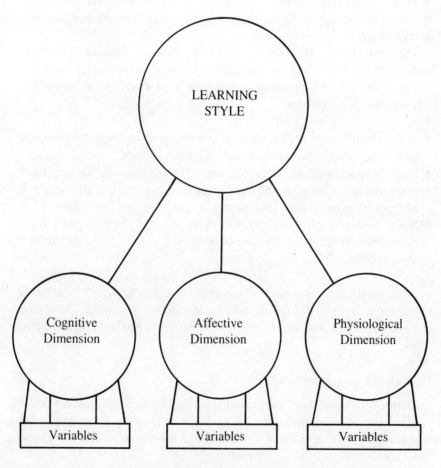

NASSP Learning Styles Task Force
Conceptual Model

Figure 1

Philosophical Consensus

A long-standing philosophical difference of opinion was debated by Task Force members and a compromise position agreed upon. The cognitive psychologists and the practitioner-oriented members of the group differed over the relative merits of remediational versus adaptational approaches to style. The adaptationists argued for changing only the learning environment, not retraining the child. This group stressed the value of individual differences and stylistic variations, recommending that emphasis be placed on a variety of learning environments, multiple resources, variable instructional methodologies, and flexible teaching.

The psychologists, on the other hand, stressed the importance of retraining learner cognitive skills for coping with the existing learning environment. Contending that some cognitive skills are more productive of school achievement than others, this group argued that sometimes learner skills needed to be augmented (remediated) for any real learning to take place.

The Task Force, after much discussion, acknowledged the validity of both positions depending on the learner's age, developmental maturity, and level of skill. Members agreed that the Task Force should support a compromise point of view.

- All students can benefit both from a responsive learning environment and from the enhancement of their learning skills.
- Some students will require more augmentation than adaptation. Their cognitive skills are unproductive; changes in learning environment will not much improve their learning.
- Some students with basically sound cognitive skills will profit from careful matching of the learning environment to their personal learning style profile.

Augmentation is more suited to cognitive style "growth"; adaptation to affective and physiological style "matching." In general, then, you augment the cognitive and adapt the affective and physiological (Keefe, 1984).

Instrument Development

During 1983, the Task Force reviewed the literature, prepared a set of concept papers, and agreed to develop a new learning style instrument that would reflect the best of current research—a state-of-the-art assessment tool.

The *Learning Style Profile* (LSP) was developed in four phases from the fall of 1983 to early 1986. Three University Centers, (Vermont, Ohio State, St. John's) developed and piloted 424 items in three domains. During the spring of 1984, separate cognitive, affective, and environmental instruments were administered regionally and an initial exploratory factor analysis conducted. The Task Force carefully reviewed these data and prepared the first draft of a unified *Profile*. Three forms consisting of some 280 surviving items were given to 625 students and a second factor analysis performed. A second draft of the *Profile* was formulated that included 142 items and 27 style factors.

The second version of the instrument was administered to 1,500 students in 15 schools and again subjected to factor analysis. A few items were eliminated to shorten and strengthen the scales. One group of items was replaced by a more reliable set, and a scale with an unreliable response set was relegated to experimental status. A final draft of 126 items was administered to a national normative sample of 5,000 students in more than 40 schools throughout the nation. Additional studies were conducted to examine the validity, reliability, and usability of the instrument.

At each stage of the development, readability checks were made, using the Dale-Chall Readability Formula. The readability of the *Learning Style Profile* was set at grades 5-6 and affirmed by six selected samples. Separate studies examined test-retest reliability and the concurrent validity of the *Profile* against the *Group Embedded Figures Test* (analytic-nonanalytic skill), *Edmonds Learning Style Identification Exercise* (for perceptual responses), and the Dunn, Dunn, and Price *Learning Style Inventory* (for affective and environmental elements).

The extensive readability checks, reliability and validity studies, and factor analyses of the instrument, combined with the supervisory efforts of the Learning Styles Task Force, strongly support the use of the *Learning Style Profile* with students in the sixth to twelfth grades. The average (internal consistency) reliability for subscales is 0.61, with a range from 0.47 to 0.76. These reliabilities are acceptable for short tests specifically intended to collect initial diagnostic information. (Since reliability is largely a function of the *length* of a test or subtest, longer subtests with similar items would provide considerably higher reliabilities.)

Profile Subscales

The NASSP *Learning Style Profile* (Keefe and Monk, 1986) in its published form profiles 24 independent subscales representing *four higher order factors:* cognitive skills, perceptual responses, study, and instructional preferences. Eight cognitive styles are assessed, three perceptual responses, and 13 study or instructional preferences.

The Task Force's conceptual model of cognitive, affective, and physiological/environmental style dimensions (Keefe, 1979) was supported, in part, by factor analytic investigation of the *Learning Style Profile* items. These first-order analyses identified eight cognitive styles, three perceptual responses, two motivational orientations (persistence and verbal risk), and 11 environmental preferences. Second-order factor analyses of the LSP subscales, however, evidenced a slightly different factor structure. The four research-based factors are as follows:

1. Seven cognitive or information processing elements (spatial, analytic, sequential processing, memory, simultaneous processing, discrimination, verbal-spatial). Categorization subscale data were not available for this analysis but the subscale clearly would load with the cognitive elements.
2. Six study preferences (mobility, posture, persistence, sound, afternoon study time, lighting). Evening preference did not load in this analysis but may be thought of as a study preference.
3. Three perceptual responses (visual, emotive, auditory).
4. Six instructional preferences (early morning time, late morning time, verbal risk, manipulative, grouping, temperature).

From a teaching-learning perspective, it is probably defensible to simplify this research model of style somewhat to think in terms of cognitive skills, perceptual responses, and study and instructional preferences.

The *Learning Style Profile* contains the following subscales, organized here by the higher order factors or dimensions.

COGNITIVE SKILLS

1. *Analytic Skill (AS)* is the capability of identifying figures concealed (embedded) in a complex background field. Persons high in this skill excel in separating a part from a whole, and in using the critical element of a problem in a different way—processes that are particularly important in such fields as mathematics and the sciences.
2. *Spatial Skill (SS)* assesses two generally accepted components of spatial reasoning—pattern recognition and spatial rotation. Pattern recognition is the capability of identifying a pattern, remembering it, and discriminating it from other similar patterns. Spatial rotation is the capacity to rotate objects in the imagination. Some evidence links spatial reasoning skill with success in aspects of mathematics, in technical courses, and in related occupations.
3. *Discrimination Skill (DS)* is the capability of focusing attention on the required dimensions of a task and avoiding distractions. This subscale, modeled on the cognitive style of focusing/scanning, involves skill in deploying attention, alertness to relevant details, and visualization of the important elements of a task.
4. *Categorization Skill (CS)* assesses variations in categorizing behavior. Narrow categorizers tend to use more complete and more accurate categories to classify information. Broad categorizers lack accuracy and organization in these tasks. Differences in categorizing behavior seem to devolve on the willingness to make judgments

about the similarity of objects or situations. The subscale measures the learner's comfort zone in making estimations and in creating adequate categories for new information.

5. *Sequential Processing Skill (SQP)* refers to a learner's capability or bias for processing information in a step-by-step, linear fashion. Sequential processing involves representations of experience that are ordered serially or temporally. Verbal processing, for example, is sequential, but a sequential task need not be verbal. Any step-by-step process (like mathematical computation) qualifies. Persons high on this subscale excel in or prefer verbal and other linear modes of processing.

6. *Simultaneous Processing Skill (SMP)* is the capability or bias for integrating the separate elements of experience into a whole, or gestalt. Simultaneous processing often has a strong spatial or visual component but the task does not have to be spatial. The essential characteristic of this kind of processing is that the entire meaning of an experience is grasped at once. Persons high on this subscale are skilled in nonverbal, figural tasks requiring the grasping of a spatial or visual gestalt.[1]

7. *Memory Skill (MS)* is based on the cognitive style of leveling vs. sharpening. Sharpeners show strength in differentiating new information from old; levelers do not. The subscale assesses a learner's capacity to retain an image of a complex figure long enough to make judgments about the similarity or difference of subsequent versions of the figure. The key element here is the capability of retaining distinct rather than vague images in repeated tasks—to detect and identify subtle changes in information.

8. *Verbal-Spatial Preference (VSP)* loads with the cognitive factors in subscale analysis. This subscale assesses a learner's preference for the verbal or spatial. It seems to tap a student's conceptual orientation for dealing with verbal or spatial *tasks*. The subscale grew out of exploratory factor analysis of test items representing preferences for learning from visual rather than verbal stimuli (e.g., films rather than books). Verbal vs. spatial preference may or may not be related to sequential or simultaneous processing skill, or to visual, auditory, or emotive perceptual response. These subscales are all highly independent. Sequential/simultaneous skills and the perceptual responses are biases in information processing or perception. Verbal-spatial preference focuses on the task itself.

---

1. The simultaneous processing subscale is experimental. Student scores are not reported on this subscale because of its poor inter-item correlations (internal consistency). New items are currently being validated.

PERCEPTUAL RESPONSES

9. *Visual Perceptual Response (VPR)* characterizes the learner who tends to respond to new information in a visual or pictorial fashion. Perception is the individual's immediate reaction to sensory stimuli. Visual perceptual response reflects a bias for learning from visual stimuli. Visual learners prefer visual, pictorial, or graphic representations of experience.

10. *Auditory Perceptual Response (APR)* characterizes the learner who responds to new information in an auditory or listening fashion. Auditory perceptual response reflects a bias for learning from auditory stimuli. Auditory listeners like to listen to others talk about experience.

11. *Emotive Perceptual Response (EPR)* characterizes the learner who responds to new information in terms of its feeling. Emotive learners react initially to the physiological or emotional tone of an experience.

STUDY AND INSTRUCTIONAL PREFERENCES

12. *Persistence Orientation (PO)* is the willingness to sustain behavior beyond the required time, to withstand discomfort, and to face the prospect of failure. High persistence is characterized by the disposition to work at a task until completion, seeking whatever help is needed to persevere. The low persistent learner usually has a short attention span and gives up easily on demanding tasks.

13. *Verbal Risk Orientation (VRO)* measures a student's willingness to verbalize, to speak out, and to state opinions even if others disagree. The subscale emerged from exploratory factor analysis of items representing physical or mental risk taking, tolerance for anxiety, and an active/reflective dimension similar to the "extraversion/introversion" scales of the Myers Briggs Type Indicator. The verbally risk-oriented learner is comfortable speaking out and defending his/her own thoughts and ideas.

14. *Manipulative Preference (MNP)* characterizes the learner who likes "hands-on" learning activities. The subscale arose from exploratory factor analysis of items written to assess tactile and kinesthetic modality preferences, but no correlation exists between this subscale and the Visual, Auditory, and Emotive Perceptual Response subscales. Manipulative learners apparently like to build, fix, make, or put things together regardless of whether their initial perceptual response is visual, auditory, or emotive. Manipulative preference likely assesses orientation to *task* while perceptual response measures orientation to *stimulus*.

Study Time Preferences are individual chronobiological predispositions deriving from the natural rhythms of the body (i.e., circadian rhythms, early childhood sleeping and waking patterns, and temperature variations). Students are more or less ready to learn depending on the time of the day.

15. *Early Morning Preference (EMP)* characterizes preference for studying and learning in the early morning.

16. *Late Morning Preference (LMP)* characterizes preference for studying and learning in the late morning.

17. *Afternoon Preference (AP)* characterizes preference for studying and learning in the afternoon.

18. *Evening Preference (EP)* characterizes preference for studying and learning in the evening.

19. *Grouping Preference (GP)* measures individual preferences for whole class, small group, or dyadic learning groups. Learning preference patterns depend, in part, on subject matter, learner attitudes and motivation, teacher characteristics, and classroom environment. A psychological need for affiliation may be the root of these preferences. The effect on achievement of matched and mismatched student grouping preferences seems to depend greatly on student attitudes toward subject and self.

20. *Posture Preference (PP)* characterizes learner bent for formal or informal study arrangements and related bodily postures. A student who prefers a formal arrangement will choose to work in an upright posture at a desk or table, using a traditional chair. A student with informal preferences will choose a more relaxed posture such as sitting or sprawling on the carpeted floor, a sofa, or an upholstered chair.

21. *Mobility Preference (MBP)* describes learner tendency to move about and take breaks while studying, or to work until the task is finished. Many researchers identify high need for mobility with hyperactivity. Others see mobility as a normal and instinctive behavior of learners reacting to unchallenging learning environments. This subscale shows a modest negative correlation with Persistence Orientation (-.30) and formal Posture Preference (-.29). It may be both age-and-sex related, since younger learners and males seem to prefer greater mobility.

22. *Sound Preference (SP)* characterizes variations in reacting to auditory stimulation. Some learners have a need for quiet, while others use moderate background sound as a screen against other distractions. The key element in "sound as screen" seems to be the level of distractability. Moderate background sound is appealing to many learners but almost no one learns well with excessive noise or obtrusive contemporary music.

23. *Lighting Preference (LP)* describes a learner's need for higher or lower levels of illumination. Bright light causes agitation or nervousness in some learners. Dim light occasions drowsiness in others. Preferences for studying in either brightly or dimly lighted areas are

highly personal and affect students' physical, emotional, and cognitive functioning.

24. *Temperature Preference (TP)* characterizes a learner's choice to study in a warm or cool setting. Even small changes in temperature can significantly affect a student's motivation to study and learn. Some researchers argue that temperature and pressure senses within the body constitute a sixth perceptual system, the homeostatic system.

Implications for Practice

Existing research suggests that students with very strong or very weak learning style controls, responses, or preferences are particularly amenable to training or instructional arrangements that optimize those responses or preferences. Students with strong cognitive skills, for example, are more ready for challenging instruction and are more capable of working at or beyond grade level. The *Learning Style Profile* helps to identify these and other important learning needs and conditions.

The LSP generates both individual and group profiles, group or class rosters, and flag rosters. The individual and group profiles report and graph each of the subscale standard scores. The class rosters provide a comprehensive listing of all scores for each student in each class. The flag rosters use a set of abbreviations to "flag" extreme scores on any subscale.

The standard computer scoring programs generate individual profiles and group rosters. Class and flag rosters can also be produced easily if a school (or district) assigns class identification codes before testing. Figures 2-4 give computer printouts of sample individual and class profiles, and a sample flag roster.

Teachers will find student and class profiles helpful in organizing instruction for students with similar cognitive strengths or weaknesses, perceptual response tendencies, or instructional preferences. Students with Analytic Skill and Categorization Skill deficiencies, for example, will need some focused problem solving training. Those with afternoon or evening Study Time preferences will function better in the morning with matched instructional and study preferences. Those with low Verbal Risk orientation will fare better in smaller groups where embarrassment is minimized and interaction can be optimized.

Flag rosters highlight only those subscale scores that fall at the extremes of response. The flags point out those students that have weak to very weak or strong to very strong skills or preferences. The mid-range of response is deliberately omitted to emphasize the dominant tendencies within a group. Students with strong visual responses, for example, are less likely to learn if instruction is strictly verbal (lecture or question-and-answer). Those with strong emotive responses or high need for "hands-on'' activities may disdain typical auditory or visual instruction. Those with strong study time or instructional preferences will learn best under personalized or matched learning conditions.

A Sample Profile

The following pages contain a set of sample items very much like those on the NASSP *Learning Style Profile*. These items are not as discriminating as those on the *Profile* but they do convey the type and format of the actual items in a straightforward way. Three cognitive skills are represented here (Analytic, Spatial, and Discrimination) and three typical study or instructional preferences (Persistence, Verbal Risk, Manipulative). Seven or more correct answers among the first nine items would suggest strong cognitive skills. The final items are self-explanatory. Answers to the questions will be found on the final page of the instrument.

Figure 2. Individual Learning Style Profile
Learning Style Profile

This profile is for: Boris Sherry A

Birthdate: 5/17/73   Sex: F   Grade: 7 Race: W

Date: 2/12/86   School: 21000   Class: 20

Skills—General Approach to Processing Information

	Score	Weak		Average	Strong
Analytic	62				xxxx
Spatial	35	xxxx			
Discrimination	38		xxxx		
Categorization	46			xxxx	
Sequential	33	xxxx			
Memory	26	xxxx			

Perceptual Responses—Initial Response to Verbal Information

	Score	Weak		Average	Strong
Visual	55			xxxx	
Auditory	43		xxxx		
Emotive	50			xxxxx	

Orientations and Preferences—Preferred Response to Study or Instructional Environment

	Score	Low		Average	High
Persistence	39	xxxx			
Verbal Risk	47			xxxx	
Manipulative	42		xxxx		

Study Time:		Low		Average	High
Early Morning	51			xxxxx	
Late Morning	52			xxxxx	
Afternoon	44			xxxx	
Evening	38	xxxx			

	Score		High	Neutral	High	
Verbal-Spatial	**	Spatial		Missing		Verbal
Grouping	36	Small	xx			Large
Posture	47	Informal		xx		Formal
Mobility	43	Stillness	xx			Movement
Sound	46	Quiet		xx		Sound
Lighting	54	Dim			xx	Bright
Temperature	40	Cool	xx			Warm

Consistency Score: 3   Normative Sample: 1986—National

NASSP—National Association of Secondary School Principals, Reston, Va.

Figure 3. Class (or Group) Learning Style Profile
Learning Style Profile

This profile is for: All Class Members

Date: 2/12/86   School: 21000   Class: 20

Skills—General Approach to Processing Information

	Score	Weak	Average	Strong
Analytic	49		xxxxx	
Spatial	56		xxxx	
Discrimination	42	xxxx		
Categorization	46	xxxx		
Sequential	51		xxxxx	
Memory	51		xxxxx	

Perceptual Responses—Initial Response to Verbal Information

	Score	Weak	Average	Strong
Visual	49		xxxxx	
Auditory	46	xxxx		
Emotive	50		xxxxx	

Orientations and Preferences—Preferred Response to Study or Instructional Environment

	Score	Low	Average	High
Persistence	47		xxxx	
Verbal Risk	49		xxxxx	
Manipulative	47		xxxx	

Study Time:

	Score	Low	Average	High
Early Morning	50		xxxxx	
Late Morning	50		xxxxx	
Afternoon	49		xxxxx	
Evening	46	xxxx		

	Score		High	Neutral	High	
Verbal-Spatial	31	Spatial	xx			Verbal
Grouping	38	Small	xx			Large
Posture	52	Informal		xxxxx		Formal
Mobility	49	Stillness		xxxxx		Movement
Sound	49	Quiet		xxxxx		Sound
Lighting	46	Dim		xx		Bright
Temperature	45	Cool		xx		Warm

Consistency Score: 3   Normative Sample: 1986—National

NASSP—National Association of Secondary School Principals, Reston, Va.

Figure 4. Flag Roster

NASSP Learning Style Profile Class Flag Roster

Date: 2/12/86   School: 21000   Class: 20

Name	Skills						Perceptual Response			Orientations						Study Time Pref.	Other Preferences							Cons
	AN	SP	DI	CA	SE	ME	VI	AU	EM	PE	VR	MA	EM	LM	AF	EV	VS	GR	PO	MO	SO	LI	TE	
Armbrewster John L	S	S	W			W				H	H		H	H		L	—	S	I					3
Boris Sherry A	S	W	W		W	WW				L							—	S			Q		C	3
Bradley Christine M					W	WW				L	H			L			—		I			D		4
Daniels Chris A	S	S	W				WW	S				H		H			—	S	I			D		2
Iberman Dianna R							WW	WW	WW		L				H		—	S			Q	D	C	3
Jones Nick G			W			S			S				L	L		L	—		F		S			3
Kent Peter		S	W			S											—		F	M	Q			8
Lawson Jessica D				W								LL	L				—	S			S	B	C	2
Leeks Shari A			WW	W		S						L	L	L		L	—	S	F	M	Q	D		4
Leplace Tiffany L	W	S	W				S			L	HH	LL	L	L			S	SS	I		S		C	5
Loxley Jennifer A		S	WW				S	W	W	L	L	LL	L	LL	LL			S		M	S			8
Maxton Jimmy L	S	S	WW				S	W					H	H	H		S	S	F		Q			5
Milton Shelly J	S	S					S	WW			LL	LL		H			S	SS	F	S	Q			2
Purdy James M	S		W				WW	S	W	L			L	H			S	S	F		S			2
Rock Richard R	W			W														S		S				1
Saylor Sharon LK	W	S						S	W	H			L		H		S	S	F	S		D		2
Schmit Daniel S	S	S				SS				L	L			H		L	S	S			Q	D	W	6
Settner Lilly K						W				H	L	L	L	L				S			S	D		3
Smith David D															L									7
Storke Jimmy K	S		W					W	W	LL	H	L	H	L	H	L	S	S	I		S	D	C	3
Tod Allison K	W	S	WW			SS	W	S		H							S	S				BB		2
Vargus R Charles	W		W			W													F		Q			10
Wilson Aaron D																	S	S						3
Wist, Lilly D		S	WW	W		SS											S	S						1
All Class Members		S	WW	W		SS											S	S			Q		C	3

Abbreviations Used on Class Rosters and Class Flag Rosters

Subscale	Abbreviation	Flags Used on Flag Roster			
		Weak		**Strong**	
Skills:					
Analytic	AN	WW	W	S	SS
Spatial	SP	WW	W	S	SS
Discrimination	DI	WW	W	S	SS
Categorization	CA	WW	W	S	SS
Sequential	SE	WW	W	S	SS
Memory	ME	WW	W	S	SS
Perceptual Responses:		**Weak**		**Strong**	
Visual	VI	WW	W	S	SS
Auditory	AU	WW	W	S	SS
Emotive	EM	WW	W	S	SS

Orientations and Preferences:

Subscale	Abbr.	Low			High	
Persistence	PE		LL	L	H	HH
Verbal Risk	VR		LL	L	H	HH
Manipulative	MA		LL	L	H	HH
Study Time:						
Early Morning	EM		LL	L	H	HH
Late Morning	LM		LL	L	H	HH
Afternoon	AF		LL	L	H	HH
Evening	EV		LL	L	H	HH
Verbal-Spatial	VS	Spatial SS	S	V	VV	Verbal
Grouping	GR	Small SS	S	L	LL	Large
Posture	PO	Informal II	I	F	FF	Formal
Mobility	MO	Stillness SS	S	M	MM	Movement
Sound	SO	Quiet QQ	Q	S	SS	Sound
Lighting	LI	Dim DD	D	B	BB	Bright
Temperature	TE	Cool CC	C	W	WW	Warm

NASSP LEARNING STYLE PROFILE

Sample Questions

1. One of the forms below is hidden in the complex figure. The hidden form is the same size, same shape, and facing the same way as one of the forms below. Select the correct hidden form.

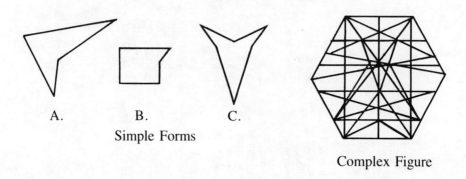

A.   B.   C.

Simple Forms

Complex Figure

How many triangles can you find in the shapes below?

2.

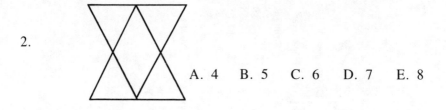

A. 4   B. 5   C. 6   D. 7   E. 8

3.

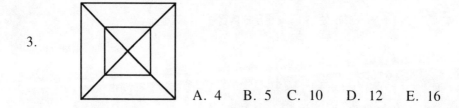

A. 4   B. 5   C. 10   D. 12   E. 16

In the center of this page is a sample circle. Compare the SIZE of the sample with the SIZE of each of the circles around it. Decide for each of the numbered circles if it is:

     A.   Smaller than the sample circle

     B.   Larger than the sample circle

     C.   The same size as the sample circle

Mark your answers below.

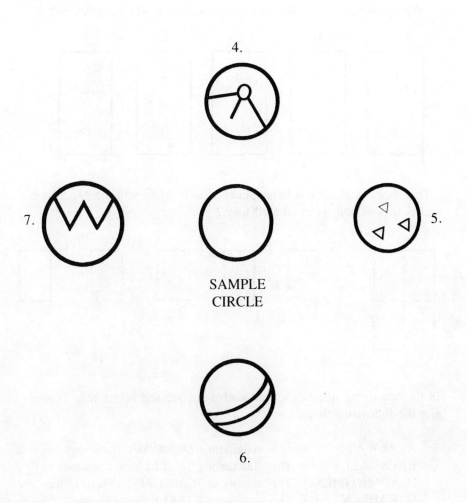

4. A   B   C   6. A   B   C

5. A   B   C   7. A   B   C

8. A piece of paper has been folded in the following ways. The star (*) shows where a part was cut out.

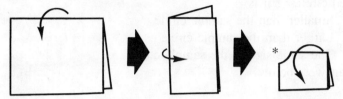

Which picture shows how the paper will look when it is unfolded?

A.   B.   C.   D.   E.

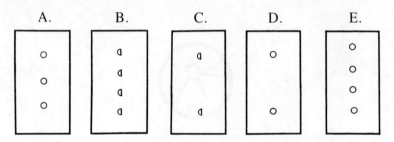

9. This sheet of paper has holes punched in it. How will the paper look after it is folded on the dotted lines?

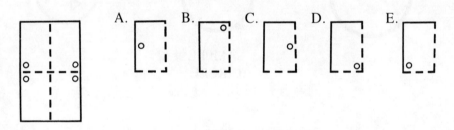

For the remaining questions, read each sentence and select your answer from the following choices:

    A. ALWAYS   —This statement *ALWAYS* describes me.
    B. USUALLY   —This statement *USUALLY* describes me.
    C. SOMETIMES —This statement *SOMETIMES* describes me.
    D. RARELY   —This statement *RARELY* describes me.
    E. NEVER   —This statement *NEVER* describes me.

10. I don't like to answer questions in class.
    A. Always   B. Usually   C. Sometimes   D. Rarely   E. Never

11. I like to put things together.
    A. Always   B. Usually   C. Sometimes   D. Rarely   E. Never

12. If I get stuck on an assignment, I give up on it.
    A. Always   B. Usually   C. Sometimes   D. Rarely   E. Never

Answers:

1. C   2. C   3. E   4. C   5. A   6. C   7. B   8. D   9. B

10. Low (ALWAYS) to high (NEVER) verbal risk

11. High (ALWAYS) to low (NEVER) preference for hands-on learning activities

12. Low (ALWAYS) to high (NEVER) persistence

References

Keefe, J.W. "Learning Style: An Overview." In *Student Learning Styles: Diagnosing and Prescribing Programs.* Reston, Va.: NASSP, 1979.

Keefe, J.W. "Education for Adaptation." Paper presented to the NASSP Learning Styles Task Force, Reston, Va., 1984.

Keefe, J.W., and Languis, M.L. "Operational Definitions." Paper presented to the NASSP Learning Styles Task Force, Reston, Va., 1983.

Keefe, J.W., and Monk, J.S. *Learning Style Profile Examiner's Manual.* Reston, Va.: NASSP, 1986.

Letteri, C.A. "Information Processing Model." Paper presented to the NASSP Learning Styles Task Force, Reston, Va., 1982.

Messick, S. *The Criterion Problem in the Evaluation of Instruction.* Princeton, N.J.: Educational Testing Service, 1969. Also in *The Evaluation of Instruction: Issues and Problems,* edited by M. Wittrock and D. Wiley. New York: Holt, Rinehart and Winston, 1970.

CHAPTER 2

The NASSP Learning Style Profile and Cognitive Processing

CHARLES A. LETTERI

EVERY EDUCATOR IS CONCERNED WITH improving the academic success of students. Educators want students to be able to learn and to apply knowledge in the various subject areas of the curriculum. And yet for all our effort, we have students who cannot learn, who are academic failures, and for whom schooling is a daily frustration.

Learning problems frequently are not related to the difficulty of the subject matter, but rather to the type and level of the cognitive processes required to learn the material. Many educators assume that students know how to learn; that they just need more motivation, or more time on task. To the contrary, recent research has clearly shown that, except in cases of physiological damage, learning disabled students have difficulty in school because they do not know the processes and operations of learning, or how to exercise control over them.

The development and use of new instruments such as the NASSP *Learning Style Profile* (LSP) make it possible for schools to diagnose the cognitive style characteristics of students, and, based on this diagnosis, design and implement specific cognitive skills training. We can now direct our efforts at the core of most learning disabilities: student deficits in the learning skills demanded by school academic tasks. We can now intervene directly in the learning process, train students to use new learning processes, and direct the transfer of these skills to new learning.

The NASSP *Learning Style Profile* is the first instrument that permits a comprehensive analysis of the learning skills and environmental preferences that affect a student's level of academic performance. The LSP assesses these skills and preferences under four major factors: Cognitive Skills, Perceptual Responses, Study Preferences, and Instructional Preferences. A complete description of each of the subscales and the meanings can be found in Chapter 1 or in the LSP *Technical Manual* (Keefe and Monk, in press).

In this chapter, I will discuss how these four factors and related subscale measures illuminate the various operations and processes of learning.

What Is Learning?

Learning is an activity of the mind that involves the application of specific and controlled operations to new information, with the result that this information becomes a part of long-term memory. The learner is central to this cognitive definition of learning. The responsibility for engaging the learning process belongs to the learner alone. The student must understand the learning process and how to control and direct it.

The ability to exercise direction and control over specific information processing operations is called Cognitive Control. When combined with other developmental, psychological, and environmental preferences of the learner, this capacity is called Learning Style. Cognition is a major component of learning style, and plays a significant role in determining the success of a student in school. Cognition refers to the various operational phases through which new information passes as the mind makes decisions about the ways that it will be represented in the student's memory.

There are six specific operational (information processing) phases that are directly related to learning:

1. Perceptual Modality
2. Perceptual Memory
3. Filter System
4. Short-Term Memory
5. Working Memory
6. Long-Term Memory

Refer to Figure 1 as we examine each of these operations and its relationship to learning.

The sources of new information can generally be thought of as external and internal. The external source encompasses all information from the student's immediate environment. The internal source includes data both about the state of the individual (e.g., hunger, thirst) and learned information stored in long-term memory (i.e., prior learning, memory of past events).

Each student has various environmental preferences that affect learning (e.g., the level of light, heat, or noise present during learning). Certain other factors such as the amount of active, hands-on learning allowed, a need for mobility, the size of the work group, and even the time of day also influence a learner's receptivity to learning and performance tasks. But no matter how conducive to learning or how supportive the environment may be, a student must possess and be able to apply specific cognitive skills to the learning task in order to achieve success.

Environmental factors may not be (often are not) optimal for each individual. Yet these same individuals usually can learn and solve problems in a most productive manner because they possess the cognitive (information processing) skills required by the task, and can transfer these skills to a wide variety of learning or performance situations.

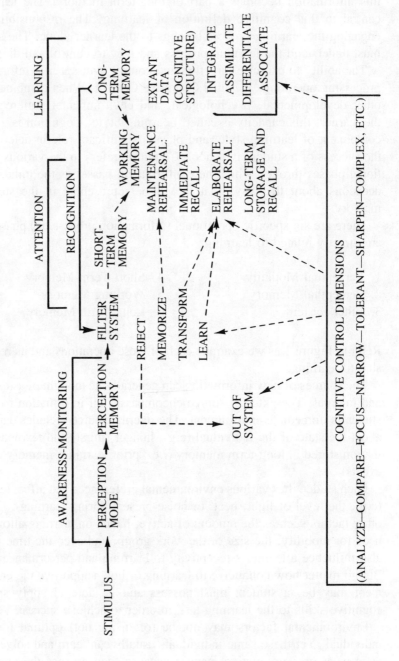

Figure 1. Information Processing, General Operations.
Charles A. Letteri, 1982

The Information Processing System

Understanding the various information processing phases is fundamental if teachers wish to provide effective instructional diagnosis and prescription. The relationship of LSP subscales to each of these phases will be highlighted in the course of the following discussion.

PERCEPTUAL MODES

External information is received by the brain through the network of perceptual modalities (eye, ear, nose, tongue, skin). This information is the raw data that the brain must process in order for learning to occur. Obviously, if a deficit exists in one of these modalities, the brain will receive incorrect or incomplete data, and limited or inappropriate learning will occur. The same is true if the data are not presented in a clear and organized fashion, or if the learner does not attend to the data as they are being presented.

The LSP measures the student's perceptual response in three modes: Visual, Auditory, and Emotive. It is important to understand a student's *initial* response mode in order to present information that is in keeping with this preference. The initial presentation of information, then, can match the student's initial response. This match provides a firmer basis for the accurate perception that is necessary for learning. (The issue of whether to match or mismatch relates to cognitive flexibility. New information calls for matching; practice or related learning for some mismatching.)

PERCEPTUAL MEMORY

The eye (sight) and the ear (hearing) each have an associated memory system called the Icon and Echo, respectively. These memory systems serve to maintain new information in an accurate format for a very brief period of time. This stage of the process appears to be necessary for the visual and auditory centers of the brain to initiate a recognition process and decide whether they know or do not know the information.

Recognition at this stage is not very important in itself, but it does provide the basis for some very important decisions to be made during the next (Filter) phase about the type and depth of processing to be performed on the information. These filtering decisions are directly related to the final disposition of the information—whether it is learned or not.

The perceptual memory phase further points out the need for assessing a student's perceptual response so that accurate representations of new information are available for further processing. The LSP measures students' initial preference for visual, auditory, or emotive response.

FILTER PHASE

The filtering system exists to prevent chaos in the processing of new information. The system serves several functions that are necessary for orderly and accurate processing. Initially, the filter automatically screens out any redundant or unwanted information so an overload does not occur in the central processing areas of working memory and long-term memory.

The central processing system is limited in the amount of information it can process and also in the amount of time allotted to processing. Not all new information received by the perceptual modalities can be processed. Chaos would result if the central processing system had to deal with all incoming information. Nothing would be processed properly.

Initial filtering and recognition seem to be automatic, but attention is not. Attention, controlled and directed by the student, is the prime prerequisite for identifying the specific information that must receive in-depth processing. If attention is not under control, inaccurate or incomplete processing will occur.

Once attention is directed to information in a controlled fashion as it passes from perceptual memory to short-term memory, decisions can be made about its final disposition. Four decisions can be made at this stage that can be repeated or changed at later stages of processing. These four decisions are to reject, to transform, to memorize, to learn.

Decision 1: To Reject

Rejection may be automatic or controlled.

Have you ever awakened in your driveway without the least recollection of going through the last two intersections? Have you ever come to the realization on a highway that you do not know whether you passed your exit or not?

These are forms of automatic rejection. You did receive the information through your sense modalities (eyes) and registered it in your perceptual memory (Icon and/or Echo), but while you were attending to your own inner thoughts (fantasies), you did not attend to the incoming information. You recognized it and even behaved in an appropriate manner, but without controlled or directed attention. So practiced are some of our behaviors that even with unattended information in perceptual memory, we can operate safely.

In other instances, we can direct the rejection at will. You might be engaged in an interesting conversation at a party. Suddenly, amid the general background noise (of which you are aware but to which you are not attending), you hear your name. You shut down your attention to the nearby conversation and try to find (with the eye and the ear) the person or the conversation with your name attached. You may even go on nodding and looking at your conversation partner, but not really attend at all.

Students do this all the time. They simply tune out instruction and attend to inner thoughts about someone or some other activity not related to the content under discussion. This is not necessarily an attentional problem, but merely a decision on the part of the learner to direct attention and the processing of information elsewhere.

An attentional deficit occurs when a learner is incapable of directing attention as required. The learner simply lacks the skill to control attention, whether to external (instruction) or internal (fantasy) information. The LSP addresses this issue under the Discrimination Skill subscale, which measures a student's capability of attending to required details and avoiding distractions.

Unless a student has the ability to direct and control attention, information at the filter phase will not be analyzed properly, and important perceptual elements will not be attended to or recognized. Learning that is disorganized and inaccurate will result. Attention at the initial presentation of information is both fundamental and critical if accurate recognition, careful identification, and organized learning are to occur.

Decision 2: To Transform

Transformation takes place when incoming information is recognized incorrectly and processed as if it were something else. A case of mistaken identity occurs. The original information is changed into something different and processed as different.

Transformation can happen when a learner selects only part of some incoming information for attention and processing. The student does not learn the authentic information, but rather some truncated and incomplete form of it. Transformations also occur when a student selects only familiar incoming information and rejects the rest. This decision reduces the cognitive load and accompanying stress, but does not result in learning. Information is processed as known or previously learned so that no change or modification is required of the existing structure in long-term memory.

Learning problems can be associated with a tendency to transform incoming information as if it were already known. This happens when a student is not aware of (or does not attend to) the distinguishing features of new information. If attention is drawn to these features, the student will recognize that the information is unique and must be processed as such. Learning will occur because the student modifies long-term memory through the addition of new and unique information.

The *Learning Style Profile* assesses these attentional and directional skills in the Discrimination, Analytic, Memory, and Categorization subscales. Students must be trained to notice and attend to the distinguishing features of new information (Discrimination) so that proper identification can be made (Analytic) and maintained (Memory) and the appropriate information modified in long-term memory (Categorization). Specifically:

- The Discrimination and Analytic Skill subscales assess the ability to focus attention on and identify the required details of information. These specific details are needed for proper learning to occur.
- The Memory Skill subscale measures the ability to retain distinct images of data as well as to notice subtle changes that occur in information over several presentations.
- The Categorization Skill subscale assesses skill in placing new information in the existing structures of long-term memory. A learner's categories must be complete and accurate, with a highly organized structure, to be of use in identifying new information or as the basis for constructing problem solutions.

A student might be required, for example, to learn and retain the distinctions among different species of mammals. While alert to the many similarities, the student notes the necessary distinctions (Discrimination and Analytic Skills) and maintains them (Memory Skill) so that accurate identifications (Categorization Skill) can be made.

In a similar way, a student reading a novel must notice and attend to (Discrimination) subtle changes in plot, time, and character development as they occur (Sequential Processing) in order to comprehend (Categorization) what is happening at any point in the story. The ability to retain distinct images of data as well as to notice subtle changes in the data (Memory) is important for this learning to be successful.

Decision 3: To Memorize

Memorization is the most frequent decision made in the processing of information. Students generally confuse memorization with learning. In fact, much of the instruction in today's classrooms emphasizes memorization as a means of demonstrating knowledge. Testing procedures stress memorizing large bodies of information. Is it any wonder that students spend huge amounts of time attempting to memorize entire chapters of textbooks (the all-night cram session)? And all this under the guise of learning!

Memorization is not learning!

Learning demands that new information modify or be added to existing information (categories) and be integrated with all related information in the student's long-term memory. Memorized information is not added to existing information, nor is it integrated in any way. It is held in isolation and requires special cues for access, recall, or reproduction. Memorized information also demands constant practice and easily falls victim to subsumption wherein its distinguishing features are lost and are no longer retrievable.

The decision to memorize new information means that it will be operated on by one of two memorizing strategies in Working Memory:

- Maintenance rehearsal
- Elaborative rehearsal.

Maintenance rehearsal is employed when information is needed only for a brief period of time and no attempt will be made to place the information in long-term memory. A typical example of maintenance rehearsal is the attempt to hold a phone number in mind while dialing. No attempt is made to place the number in long-term memory, but only to hold it long enough to finish dialing.

We know this type of memory is fragile and sensitive. Any interruption of the process (someone calling your name) will destroy the memory of the number. You must start again by looking at the number, and then repeat it over and over as you try to dial.

This constant repetition, called maintenance rehearsal, is useful for only brief storage time (several minutes) and for an extremely limited amount of information (7 +/-2 bits). Yet, this type of study procedure is used by a majority of students at all levels of schooling. It is a process introduced in the early grades for learning songs, rhymes, the alphabet, and other information to be memorized. Drill-and-practice sessions train students in the process and it is applied to all learning tasks.

Information practiced in this way, over many sessions, will eventually find its way into long-term memory, but it will have to be constantly updated and repeated for accurate recall. In addition, the information will not be integrated into existing categories (learned).

Maintenance rehearsal is a process fraught with error and instability. Students with repeated learning problems in school courses that require memorizing large amounts of data may simply not know how to memorize efficiently.

Elaborative rehearsal involves designing and applying specific organizing structures to information so that it can be placed in long-term memory with accuracy and ease of recall. These organizing structures are called mnemonics. Although specific types of mnemonics do exist, it is far more relevant and productive to teach students the procedures for *constructing* mnemonics so they can design appropriate strategies for specific materials to be memorized. In reality, mnemonics are study skills and should be taught together with the materials to be memorized.

The LSP addresses both maintenance and elaborative rehearsal skills in the Memory Skill subscale. This subscale alerts teachers to those students who likely will experience difficulty in subject areas that require memorizing large amounts of information.

Decision 4: To Learn

Learning is a decision that calls for processing new information so that it is added to or modifies existing categories of information in long-term memory.

Learning demands that the student maintain constant control and direction over the processing of new information. When presented with a new object, a student first must establish recognition by analyzing the features of the object (Analytic/Discrimination) and then scan existing information in long-term memory for a category of objects with the same features.

If this process is affirmative, the student can add the new object to the existing category as another example. If no known category exists, then the student must create one with the attended features serving as the parameters of the new category (Categorization).

The Analytic and Spatial Skill subscales of the LSP measure a student's ability to examine objects and information in a detailed and direct manner. All features of the object (Spatial) and pertinent information (Analytic) are attended to and can either be added to existing categories or used to create new categories (Categorization). If a new category, it must also be integrated with related, existing categories of information.

Learning is always a conscious, controlled, and directed cognitive activity. The student has the prime responsibility for making the decision to learn and for carrying out all the requisite operations demanded by the decision. When a decision to learn has been made, all other activity in the information processing system must be temporarily suspended to provide the cognitive space, time, and attention for processing the information (Sequential and Simultaneous Processing Skills).

A great deal of concentration is required of the student. Incidental incoming information must be ignored as well as tempting internal messages about food, drink, daydreams, etc. Students who have even the slightest attentional problems will experience great difficulty in actual learning because high levels of concentration are needed.

Circumstances can occur, however, when familiar music or comfortable surroundings may be helpful in establishing a comfortable environment and reducing the stress of learning. The LSP measures these kinds of environmental preferences in its Sound, Light, and Temperature Preference subscales.

These elements are not *directly* related to the learning process itself (cognition). The process of learning is the same for all. Information progresses from Perception and the Filter System through Short-Term and Working Memory and is integrated within the information structure of Long-Term Memory. Environmental preferences simply address the context of learning; whether it is supportive or not.

SHORT-TERM MEMORY

Short-term memory, as its name implies, exists to maintain small amounts of information for brief periods of time. Maintenance time can be dramatically increased by constant and extended practice so that ''overlearning'' occurs. Overlearning helps the information find its way into long-term memory, but information ''learned'' in this way is not integrated into the network of existing cognitive categories. The information requires periodic rehearsal and specific cues for recall. It is also prone to rapid decay and loss from memory.

Another means of increasing maintenance time and the amount of storage in short-term memory is through such mnemonic devices as chunking and grouping. To memorize the names of the primary colors, a student can take the first letter of each color and make a name of them: R (red) O (orange) Y (yellow) G (green) B (blue) I (indigo) V (violet) = Roy G. Biv. A similar mnemonic would be the letter designations for remembering the lines and spaces of a musical clef: Every Good Boy Does Fine (EGBDF) and FACE.

Chunking reduces the number of bits of information that must be memorized and adds some ''sense'' to the organization. This added level of meaning makes the information easier to organize and provides a salient cue for access and recall when needed. (Remember that this information must be constantly practiced or it will be lost to access and recall.) Short-term memory's most important function is to maintain information long enough for working memory to apply the appropriate operations for real learning to occur.

WORKING MEMORY

Working memory is not a storage area for information like Short or Long-Term Memory. Rather, it is a function and process that allows information being maintained in Short-Term Memory and the appropriate cognitive operations and structures of Long-Term Memory to be brought together. Only information from short-term memory and those processes required for elaborative rehearsal (memorizing) or assimilation and integration (learning) are present in Working Memory. All other information is lost to the system (rejected), changed so that learning is not required (transformed), or used and then lost (maintenance rehearsal).

We have enormous amounts of information in our long-term memories, but these data are only a minute fraction of the information that has been received and partially processed by the information processing system. Incoming information is subjected to a wide variety of cognitive operations and procedures, some of which are not under the direct control of the individual.

This complexity contributes to the extreme fragility of the information. Attention to incoming information (Discrimination Skill) as well as direction for the processes (Sequential and Simultaneous Processing) are necessary so that the information approaches the final phase of processing (Memory Skill) with enough stability to become a distinct part of the cognitive structure (Categorization Skill).

LONG-TERM MEMORY

Long-term memory contains everything we have ever learned (semantic) or experienced (episodic), in a more or less accessible and organized fashion. Useful placement in long-term memory requires that information be:

1. Learned
2. Organized while being learned, and
3. Integrated into existing cognitive structures.

If these basic conditions are not met, long-term memory becomes nothing more than a haphazard accumulation of highly disorganized and loosely related information.

In addition to accumulated knowledge and experience, long-term memory also contains general rules and principles of learning, and content-specific principles and procedures. *Content-specific procedures* are operations required for learning and solving problems in specific subject matter. Typical examples would include knowing the sequences to follow in solving different kinds of math problems; or how to determine an accurate sequence of objects by size; or how to count.

In a math unit, for example, a student might be asked to solve the equation: $2 (4+2) + 3 (6-4) = ?$

Cognitive-specific procedures involved in the solution are:

1. Addition
2. Subtraction
3. Multiplication

4. Solve inside paranthesis first
5. Proceed from left to right
6. Place solution to right of $=$ sign

Content-specific principles represented are (in part):

- The One-to-One Principle—one number is assigned to objects in a set or series.
- The Stable Order Principle—numbers have a specific and unchanging sequence.
- The Abstraction Principle—any series of items, concrete or abstract, can be counted.

It should be apparent from this brief outline that even rudimentary mathematical operations demand a variety of understandings and operations. Not all learners have these understandings or are equally capable of the operations. Cognitive training programs can equalize some of this imbalance and help students raise their achievement in all areas of the curriculum.

Processes for the application of *general cognitive rules and operations* also are an important part of long-term storage. These generic information processing rules and operations are never taught in themselves.

The learner extracts them from ongoing learning or training activities (implicit learning).

Implicit learning takes place from the moment of birth as a result of interactions with the environment and the significant others in our lives. Typical examples are the rules of syntax and grammar for the native language or social conventions reflecting one's culture.

Cognitive controls, for example, are not an explicit part of the school curriculum. Teachers assume that students have these skills, but research affirms that the majority do not. Cognitive controls are the basic skills that students can learn or be trained to use to control the operations of their information processing systems.

Many students do not know how to use these controls so learning, for them, is a chancy affair. They have great difficulty in placing new information in their long-term memories in an organized and integrated way. Other students who have mastered the controls have highly organized and accessible structures of knowledge in long-term memory. They learn at increasing levels that are both faster and greater in the amount learned and retained.

Students learn the subtle ability to control thinking procedures (and the related rules) in the same manner as language. The process starts immediately after birth and reflects the kind of environment in which the child is raised. If these rules and principles are not learned implicitly from the significant others, they must be learned in an explicit fashion. The learner must be taught the skills, given practice in their use, and guidance and training in their transfer.

In fact, the learner must learn how to think and learn.

These generic learning skills are the bases for academic achievement, yet they are rarely addressed directly in most schools or classrooms. Since the operations are largely self-taught, great variance exists in the skill levels of individual students. Students without the skills are open to failure, and their teachers are subject to frustration in attempts to assist them.

Here the value of the *Learning Style Profile* becomes most evident. The LSP provides teachers with information about student learning style (specific skills, capabilities, and preferences) and guides them in creating specific training programs for their students.

The Challenge

Training in the operations and controls required for learning must be an integral part of any educational program. Since students are ultimately responsible for their own learning, they must learn to control and direct the operations necessary to establish in long-term memory the organized structures for learning. Cognitive skills (and their training) are prerequisites for successful student achievement.

The NASSP *Learning Style Profile* and its referent science of information processing are the latest advances in the field of education. The instrument profiles the levels of student cognitive skills and provides a basis for the development of relevant intervention and training programs. It remains for the education profession to make profitable use of these advances in assessment and training in order to support significant improvement in our schools.

References

Bourne, L.E., Edkstrand, R.B.; and Dominowslo, R.L. *The Psychology of Thinking*. Englewood Cliffs, N.J.: Prentice Hall, 1971.

Bruner, J.S., and Tajfel, H. "Cognitive Risk and Environmental Change." *Journal of Abnormal Psychology* 62(1961):231-241.

Gardner, R.W.; Holzman, P.S.; Klein, G.S.; Linton, H.B., and Spence, D. "Cognitive Control: A Study of Individual Consistencies in Cognitive Behavior." *Psychological Issues* 4(1959):1-185.

Gardner, R.W., and Long, R.I. "Control Defense and Centration Effect: A Study of Scanning Behavior." *British Journal of Psychology* 53(1962):129-140.

Holzman, P.S. "Scanning: A Principle of Reality Contact." *Perceptual and Motor Skills* 23(1960):835-844.

Kagan, J. "Impulsive and Reflective Children: Significance in Conceptual Tempo." In *Learning and the Educational Process*, edited by J.D. Krumboltz. Chicago: Rand McNally, 1965.

Kelly, G.A. *The Psychology of Personal Constructs*. New York: Morton and Co., 1955.

Klatzky, R.L. *Human Memory: Structures and Process*. San Francisco: W.H. Freeman, 1980.

Klein, G.S.; Gardner, R.W.; and Schlesinger, N.J. "Tolerance for Unrealistic Experience: A Study of the Generality of a Cognitive Control." *British Journal of Psychology* 53(1962):41-55.

Letteri, C.A. "Cognitive Profiles: Basic Determinant of Academic Achievement." *Journal of Education Research* 73(1982): 195-199.

————. "Cognitive Profiles: Relationship to Achievement and Academic Success." In *Student Learning Styles and Brain Behavior: Programs, Instruments, Research*. Reston, Va.: NASSP, 1982.

————. "Teaching Students How To Learn." *Theory into Practice* 35(1985).

Pettigrew, T.F. "The Measurement and Correlates of Category Width as a Cognitive Variable." *Journal of Personality* 26(1958).

Travers, R.M.W. *Essentials of Learning*. New York: Macmillan, 1982.

CHAPTER 3

Using the NASSP Learning Style Profile

BARBARA FERRELL

IT IS CHRISTMAS EVE. Our daughter has finally gone to bed and it is time for us to put the present from Santa under the tree. This year, it's a bicycle.

It is now almost midnight. We pull the box with the bicycle out of the attic and open the box; but, instead of a complete bicycle like the one we selected from the rack in the department store, we find a box of bicycle parts.

A white sheet of paper, the "Instructions," falls to the floor with the rest of the pieces. I pick up the paper and begin to read. "Take the front wheel and position it in the fork of the frame." By the time I turn around to follow this instruction, I see that my husband has already attached the front wheel to the frame and is putting together a number of the other parts.

This scenario may be familiar to you. It is an example of how differences in learning style, like those measured by the NASSP *Learning Style Profile,* affect our lives, even outside the educational setting.

Since the term "learning style" was first coined by Herb Thelen in 1954, two things have become apparent about learning style from research in the field: individual differences in learning style do exist; and, when efforts are made to match an individual's learning style with an instructional environment, the outcomes of learning are positively affected.

Learning style research historically has been handicapped by problems with the instrumentation available to measure the wide variety of learning style constructs. Instrumentation has been limited in the breadth of its coverage, the age levels for which the measures were developed, and the psychometric soundness of the assessment methods employed.

These kinds of limitations prompted the NASSP to convene the Learning Styles Task Force, which developed the *Learning Style Profile.* The instrument directly addresses all the critical areas of concern. It measures 24 style elements, is specifically geared for use in middle level and senior high schools (where test development was particularly weak), is valid and reliable, and is normed on a national sample of 5,000 students. Both individual and class profiles can be generated from the LSP scores.

Now that the instrument is available, it is necessary to address its potential usefulness in the secondary school setting. This task is, in many ways, the more difficult one. The very strengths of the LSP also mirror its limitations for use in the typical school. It is necessary to consider both these strengths and limitations before establishing its utility. (It may be impossible to separate them in actual use.)

1. The LSP is a new instrument. Its potential value is, for the most part, still to be documented by its users. Yet, the instrument is based on the enormous body of learning style research that preceded it. Research that applies to many earlier learning style constructs has relevance for the 24 subscales of the LSP. We can also suggest applications based on this wealth of data. Some of this information base will be discussed later.
2. Normative data for the LSP are available for a relatively large sample, but this sample represents a general one. No normative data are yet available for special populations that a school may wish to assess. This means that school norms may need to be established. (LSP computer scoring programs do control for sex, grade, and racial variations.)
3. The task force has consistently conceptualized the LSP within a broader framework—an overall assessment model. In this context, the LSP is a "first level" diagnostic. The instrument deliberately covers a broad spectrum of learning style constructs, so each subscale has relatively few items. The reliabilities of these subscales are limited by their length. As a result, the interpretation of results should be approached conservatively.

The task force envisioned the LSP being given to all students in a school to provide baseline diagnostic information (level one). Clinical measures, administered at the school by trained personnel such as counselors, would comprise a second level. Tests designed to measure a single construct of the 24 represented on the LSP could be given to students who scored at either extreme of any of the subscales. A student who scored low on the Analytic Skills subscale, for example, could be given the *Group Embedded Figures Test* as a follow-up. Clinical referral and assessment would represent a third level, one appropriate for only a very small percentage of the students in a given school.

In the following sections, I will explore ways that information from the LSP can be used to focus on the learning of individual students, on classroom groups, or on the whole population of the school.

Individual Student Focus

Profiling individual students might seem to be the simplest use of the LSP, but it is by no means the least important. At this level of application, a school administrator or teacher could administer the LSP to a single student, a group of students, or the whole school population, and share the results only with the individuals tested. The individual student profile would be used to report the results and each student would learn about his or her own range of skills and preferences. (See p. 14 in Chapter 1 for a sample profile.)

Individual style reporting raises student awareness of the different ways individuals learn and the fact that these differences carry with them no judgment of right or wrong. Students who prefer to work alone, for example, and those who prefer larger groups both have acceptable preferences.

At this level of application, someone at the school—a teacher or perhaps a counselor—would interpret the profile for the student. The various subscales could be explained and each student helped to understand where his or her scores fall in relation to others taking the test.

This level of application is particularly important for student self-awareness and academic motivation. As a child, I always thought there was something wrong with my eyes because I preferred to work at low levels of illumination. It was only when I began to learn about environmental preferences that I realized my "peculiarity" was acceptable and merely an expression of my learning style.

Information from a student's individual profile also could be used to plan educational programs. Many relationships have been found between the various learning style constructs measured by the LSP and the types of academic majors that students choose in college.

David Kolb (Kolb, Rubin, and McIntyre, 1979), for example, found that physics, mathematics, and chemistry majors scored high on the abstract dimension of his instrument (LSP Analytic Skill). He postulated that many student changes in major were due to "fundamental mismatches between personal learning styles and the learning demands of different disciplines." Mismatches between learning style preference and career choices may also account for dissatisfaction with the workplace.

Information about learning style preferences may help a student understand that a mismatch may exist between a student's preferred style and the way a teacher teaches a class. This type of information can help students understand conflicts with teachers, or with other students in the class. A logical extension of the "match/mismatch" concept would be to motivate students to "stretch" their own styles of learning (Gregorc, 1979), and to increase their preferred repertoire of learning tools or learning environments.

Students may not always have a learning environment that represents the ideal for them. Sometimes they must adapt in order to succeed. This "alignment" (Gregorc, 1979) is much easier for some students than for others. Indeed, it is necessary to train some students to adjust to the learning environment (cf. Chapter 2 for examples).

Teacher/Classroom Focus

Just as individual students can benefit from an awareness of learning style, so can teachers. No norms are available for adult use of the LSP, but teachers can benefit from taking the Profile. Teachers often teach in the ways that they have been taught. These "teaching styles" may not be the same as their preferred learning styles. A teacher's Profile may or may not provide clues to his or her preferred teaching style, but it unquestionably can point to any obvious differences between learning and teaching behaviors.

A knowledge of style can show teachers some of their own behaviors that can hinder student progress. The LSP class profile, for example, may show that teachers are using teaching methods that do not match the learning skills or preferences of the majority of students in a class. Class profiles can also help teachers identify learning style tendencies of a class as a whole.

A teacher who is having problems with certain group activities may find that the majority of a class prefer working in dyads or small groups (LSP Grouping Preference). The teacher can then decide whether to modify group activities or to find ways to help learners work better in the larger group. In any event, class profiles will reveal a wide variety of learning styles in a typical classroom. This knowledge will help teachers decide which instructional modes and methods to employ.

The classroom teacher, even at the senior high school level, can provide options to address student needs without changing the basic structure of the classroom. There are some things that learning styles research already tells us about such options. The LSP has three scales, for example, that assess Perceptual Response: Visual, Auditory, and Emotive. Students with an auditory preference have been found to learn best when they listen to new information first, then read or take notes. Visual students do better when they read first. By varying the instructional plan—sometimes presenting the lecture first and then giving the reading assignment, or sometimes vice versa—the teacher can reach both types of students.

Similarly, a teacher can include some small-group activities either with or without teacher involvement for those students who prefer to work in groups. Brainstorming activities in particular appeal to those who like interaction with their peers.

A knowledge of individual student Profiles can be important to classroom teachers interested in optimum learning outcomes. A student who scores low on the Verbal Risk Orientation subscale of the LSP (not willing to volunteer in class) may still score high on the LSP cognitive skill dimensions (Analytic, Spatial, Discrimination, Categorization, Sequential and Simultaneous Processing, Memory) and learn easily. Knowing that a student has a high need for mobility (LSP Mobility Preference) may explain why that student constantly has to sharpen a pencil, get drinks of water, or go to the bathroom. The teacher can structure some socially acceptable opportunities for the student to move about the room yet avoid discipline problems.

Institutional Focus

If a school makes a general commitment to implement style-based instruction based on the LSP, there are some important planning considerations and a number of directions that it may take.

A great deal of prior research on special populations is relevant to the learning style constructs assessed by the LSP. Gifted students, for example, have been shown to have certain learning style characteristics (Dunn and Price, 1980; Griggs and Price, 1980).

Studies with gifted populations have found them to be more persistent than typical students (LSP Persistence Orientation), to prefer working alone (LSP Grouping Preference), and to prefer visual learning to auditory learning (LSP Perceptual Response). Planning special programs for the gifted should take these differences into account.

For any total school implementation, whether student awareness or style matching is the goal, some planning considerations are paramount for the program to have a chance of success. Administrative backing is basic: The administration must provide a supportive climate. A teacher who makes modifications in the classroom to accommodate the learning styles of students must be sure of support. If an administrator reprimands a student who prefers an informal environment for sitting on the floor (LSP Posture Preference), or rebukes a teacher, the program is doomed to failure.

All individuals involved in the implementation, including the principal, should become as familiar as possible with the concept of learning style and with the LSP. Teachers and administrators should take the LSP to learn about their own learning styles. Inservice activities should be planned to help teachers become more flexible in their teaching strategies. Help should be available for interpreting both individual and class profiles.

Planning for a learning style-based approach in any school should include the following components:

- A policy decision by the school administration about the breadth of involvement (student, teacher/classroom, special population, whole school).
- Acquisition of materials for the professional library on learning style in general and the LSP specifically.
- Examination and pilot testing of the LSP in the school, schools, or specific groups in which the program is to be implemented.

- Development of a testing plan that includes both initial testing and strategies for testing new students.
- Establishment of a staff development program that begins with administrators and eventually includes all teachers. The program should foster awareness, provide interpretation of LSP profiles, and suggest strategies for classroom implementation.
- Formation of continuing support structures for teachers (small groups, mentor relationships, etc.)
- An evaluation component to document the progress and outcomes of the program.
- A procedure for second and perhaps third level style assessment.

References
Dunn, R., and Price, G.E. "Identifying the Learning Style Characteristics of Gifted Children." *Gifted Child Quarterly* 24(1980):33-36.

Gregorc, A.F. "Learning/Teaching Styles: Their Nature and Effects." In *Student Learning Styles: Diagnosing and Prescribing Programs.* Reston, Va.: NASSP, 1979.

Griggs, S.A., and Price, G.E. "Learning Styles of Gifted Versus Average Junior High School Students." *Phi Delta Kappan* 61(1980):361.

Kolb, D.A.; Rubin I.M.; and McIntyre, J.M. *Organizational Psychology: An Experiential Approach.* 3rd ed. Englewood Cliffs, N.J.: Prentice-Hall, 1979.

Thelen, H. *Dynamics of Groups at Work.* Chicago: University of Chicago Press, 1954.

CHAPTER 4

A Learning Style Approach to Effective Instruction

JOHN M. JENKINS

STUDENT OUTCOMES are the bottom line of a school program. The demand for higher standards, so prevalent today, may result in raising the bar higher but not in helping students vault it. The key to helping more students achieve in our schools would seem to involve offering them different ways to reach common goals. Fortunately, technology is now available to help educators do just that.

The NASSP *Learning Style Profile* provides comprehensive information about how students learn so instruction can be better adapted to their strengths or steps taken to strengthen cognitive skills. Schools, for the most part, do rather well in collecting information about *what students know*. Combining this information with profiles of the *ways students learn* offers teachers, counselors, and teacher advisers the opportunity to do a more effective job of working with individual students.

Two definitions of learning style have helped me understand the concept better. The first, from Rita and Kenneth Dunn (1978), emphasizes that learning style is the way individuals concentrate on, absorb, and retain new information or skills. In this context, concentration seems closely related to time-on-task or academic learning time; and absorbing information and retaining it seems related to what educators hope for all students in a school setting.

James Keefe and Marlin Languis (Keefe, 1985) present a more comprehensive definition of learning style which addresses the three domains of the *Learning Style Profile*. They suggest that learning style is a composite of cognitive, affective, and physiological/environmental factors that determine how students perceive, interact with, and respond to the learning environment. The elements in these three domains serve as controls and basic orientations by which students come to learn what they are asked to learn.

If the learning environment does not offer appropriate alternatives (most traditional classrooms do not), then students are forced to make the best of a less than efficacious situation. The energy they use to make adjustments may subtract from the energy available for learning. The less energy students must bring to bear on the demands of the learning environment, the more energy they will have available for learning successfully.

Students who know their learning styles have a measure of control over the events of the classroom. Teaching to learning style differences reinforces that sense of control. Research evidence indicates that when teachers begin to adjust instruction to diagnosed learning style differences, academic achievement increases, attitude toward learning is more positive, and fewer discipline problems occur.

Planning for a Learning Style Approach

In a recent book, Naisbitt and Aburdene (1985) write about changes in the corporate world designed to make the industrial setting more personal. These changes in the way industry works with individual employees are a partial response to the "megatrends" described in Naisbitt's book of the same name.

Similarly, Albert Shanker, president of the American Federation of Teachers, told the inaugural meeting of Deans of Education in the Holmes Group: "We need to create a system where students do not sit still from 9 in the morning to 3 in the afternoon writing down notes from the blackboard or lectures. Schools should be designed to tailor education to each child."

Building on the technology of the learning style movement, schools can help teachers begin to design more personalized classrooms tailored to individual students.

Several steps can be taken to introduce learning style to a school staff. The following have worked for me:

- Begin with an orientation or awareness session to give a sense of your understanding and enthusiasm for the idea.
- Spend time expanding knowledge and understanding of learning style. Become familiar with some of the research findings that support a serious application of this approach to teaching.
- Administer a learning style instrument or two to your faculty members and interpret the results for them. I like to use the *Productivity Environmental Preference Survey* (Dunn, Dunn, and Price, 1982), and the *Myers Briggs Type Indicator* (Briggs and Myers, 1977). It is also useful to have teachers take the NASSP *Learning Style Profile,* even though it is normed for middle level and high school students. (The experience is a good advance organizer for teachers.)
- Organize teachers in learning teams to give them support as they learn more about the concept of learning style. This step is particularly important when teachers begin to implement a style program. It is also appropriate for administrators to work with teachers in ways commensurate with their individual learning styles. Schedule morning meetings for some, personalize the inservice program, offer variety and choice for learning new approaches to teaching.

- Develop a schoolwide management system for implementing a learning style program. Build learning style diagnosis into your comprehensive testing program; develop a student profile format for recording salient information about individual students; start a learning style steering committee; educate and inform parents; provide budgetary support for teachers to develop materials; establish an ongoing staff development program; recognize teacher accomplishments; establish an evaluation scheme.
- Urge teachers to spend time discussing learning styles with students. It is best for teachers to present ideas informally at first. Students will come to see that differences in how people learn are normal and expected.
- Have teachers administer the NASSP *Learning Style Profile* to students. Begin with several classes or adviser groups. Provide help for teachers in interpreting the results and planning instructional strategies.

Implementing the Program

When our accomplishments fall short of our expectations, our tendency is to behave like the Avis car rental company; that is, we try harder. It would be better to work "smarter." "Smarter" classrooms are places where more students learn because teachers diagnose their strengths and weaknesses and work to design instructional environments more commensurate with their learning style characteristics.

But teachers are individuals too and differ in their readiness and ability to implement new ideas. With this in mind, it is helpful to give teachers an overview of the steps they can take to create learning style classrooms.

This chart provides such an overview.

Developmental Steps in Implementing a Learning Style Program

Phase One: Teach all students similarly but make adjustments in the learning environment (classroom).

Phase Two: Teach all students similarly but provide a variety of activities in order to match all students' learning styles at one time or another.

Phase Three: Use small/cooperative group learning strategies about 70 percent of the time as an alternative to traditional instruction.

Phase Four: Diagnose differences in learning style and prescribe cognitive skills retraining or one of several ways to learn common objectives.

All teachers can participate in "making classrooms smarter" by starting with Phase One and working systematically toward Phase Four. Phase One is a sound starting point. Adjusting for differences in environmental and physiological learning style elements costs little and can be accomplished with a minimum of effort.

Such things as preference for bright or dim light can prompt a teacher to rethink a seating chart. Time-of-day considerations can influence a counselor or a teacher adviser to schedule a student into personally demanding subjects when energy levels are highest. Posture preference can be accommodated by creating a section of the room where bean bag chairs, couches, and similar kinds of furniture replace the typical student desk.

Phase Two is a logical next step. Again, students are taught similarly but now with deliberate variety. An overhead projector can enhance the spoken word for visual students. Some manipulative (tactile and kinesthetic) activities can be introduced to help students who prefer to process information in this manner. Students can work in pairs, teams, small groups, or alone. The key at this phase is to provide different activities even though all students accomplish the same thing and in the same sequence.

Phase Three requires the design and implementation of small-group activities for the entire class. Use cooperative group strategies, team learning, brainstorming, group competition, and small-group review of previous learning. These small-group techniques adjust for many learning style differences simultaneously and are easier for secondary teachers to implement. They represent a useful prelude to a more diagnostic and prescriptive approach to teaching.

Phase Four is a truly personalized learning approach (Keefe, 1984). Student learning styles are diagnosed and the profiles used to prescribe different instructional approaches to common objectives. Students with cognitive skill deficiencies are identified and provided remedial assistance. Students with visual strengths and formal study preferences are taught one way. Manipulative learners have materials designed specifically for their style preferences.

Students with high persistence and informal learning preferences are given help in structuring their own learning activities. The classroom is rearranged and students work alone, in pairs, in learning teams, or with the teacher. All students are expected to achieve the same objectives, but are given the opportunity to do so differently.

Getting Started

Helping teachers to implement a learning style approach implies a healthy degree of staff development, practice, and support. Teachers adopt practices at different rates and with different understandings. As the instructional leader of the school, the principal is the teacher of teachers. The principal should begin with inservice opportunities designed to develop an awareness of learning style.

Discuss the NASSP *Learning Style Profile* and its 24 elements of style. Once awareness is heightened, teachers can be helped to diagnose student differences and to prescribe appropriate style-based learning activities.

As secondary schools move toward more standardized outcomes for all students, it is important to realize that higher goals are not possible unless we correspondingly develop varied ways for students to get there. The idea that one method, one teacher, or one approach to learning is valid for all students is no longer tenable.

The ideal of American education remains the same: Schools exist for all students. The developments in learning style technology during the past 10 years make it feasible for educators to come closer to this ideal. We must be open to the ideas, willing to rethink our biases, willing to try new approaches, and willing to learn in the process.

References

Briggs, K.C., and Myers, I.B. *Myers-Briggs Type Indicator*. Palo Alto, Calif.: Consulting Psychologists Press, 1977.

Dunn, R., and Dunn, K. *Teaching Students Through Their Individual Learning Styles: A Practical Approach*. Reston, Va.: Reston Publishing Co., 1978.

Dunn, R.; Dunn, K.; and Price, G.E. *Productivity Environmental Preference Survey*. Lawrence, Kans.: Price Systems, 1982.

Keefe, J.W. "Personalized Education." In *Instructional Leadership Handbook,* edited by J.W. Keefe and J.M. Jenkins. Reston, Va.: NASSP, 1984.

Keefe, J.W. "Assessment of Learning Style Variables: The NASSP Task Force Model." *Theory into Practice* XXIV (1985): 138-144.

Naisbitt, J., and Aburdene, P. *Reinventing the Corporation*. New York: Warner Books, 1985.